Pilot and Adventurer

by Ryan Frank
illustrated by Ruth Palmer

SCHOOL PUBLISHERS

Requests for permission to make copies of any part of the work should be addressed to School Permissions and Copyrights, Harcourt, Inc., 6277 Sea Harbor Drive, Orlando, Florida 32887–6777. Fax: 407-345-2418.

HARCOURT and the Harcourt Logo are trademarks of Harcourt, Inc., registered in the United States of America and/or other jurisdictions.

Printed in China

ISBN 10: 0-15-351046-3
ISBN 13: 978-0-15-351046-5

Ordering Options
ISBN 10: 0-15-350602-4 (Grade 5 On-Level Collection)
ISBN 13: 978-0-15-350602-4 (Grade 5 On-Level Collection)
ISBN 10: 0-15-357971-4 (package of 5)
ISBN 13: 978-0-15-357971-4 (package of 5)

5 6 7 8 9 10   468   12 11 10 09

A pioneer is a person who is among the first to explore something for others. A pioneer can be a great inventor who discovers a new tool. A pioneer can be a political leader who creates a new government, or a pioneer can just be someone who attempts something new and unknown. Amelia Earhart was a true pioneer. She made people think differently about flight and what it meant to be a pilot.

Amelia Mary Earhart was born on July 24, 1897, in the remote town of Atchison, Kansas. As a young girl, she did not show much interest in flying at all. In fact, when she was ten years old, she saw her first plane at a state fair, and she wasn't impressed. She thought that it looked rusty and old. It wasn't until about ten years later that she realized flying was her future.

At the age of twenty, Amelia attended a stunt flying exhibition with her friend, where they watched planes fly back and forth while the pilots performed tricks. One of the pilots in the show spotted Amelia and her friend, and he thought that he would try to scare them. He flew the plane right toward the two of them. Amelia did not move an inch. Instead, she stood her ground as the plane approached. Being around planes didn't scare her like it did most people. Planes would be an important part of her future.

Most people who knew Amelia weren't surprised to learn of her fascination with planes. Amelia had spent her whole life seeking out more adventurous activities than her peers. She enjoyed climbing trees and riding sleds.

She was particularly attracted to activities that weren't easily attainable for women at that time. In her room, she kept a scrapbook of newspaper clippings about women who had succeeded in roles that were usually reserved for men. Areas such as engineering, film direction, and law were fields in which women had to struggle to succeed. Amelia knew that women were just as capable and intelligent as men, and she set out to prove this to the world.

Amelia graduated from high school in 1915. After graduation, she went on to become a nurse's aide in Canada. During this time, World War I was taking place, and Amelia worked in a military hospital taking care of wounded soldiers. She also studied hard and attended college. Eventually, she got a job as a social worker and began to save money.

On January 3, 1921, Amelia's life would be forever changed. That was the day of her first flying lesson. After learning how to fly, Amelia decided to buy her own plane. It was a small, yellow two-seater plane that she nicknamed "Canary." It didn't take her long to get used to flying it. She was born to fly; she flew the plane to an altitude of 14,000 feet (4.3 km) almost immediately after she bought it. It was the first time a woman had ever flown that high!

Despite a new world record, Amelia was disappointed that she received so little attention. She had set a world record, but she was still not recognized as a great pilot. She continued to work as a social worker and flew her plane as a hobby.

Then in 1928, she received an urgent phone call that would change everything. The caller asked Amelia whether she would like to fly across the Atlantic Ocean. Even though Amelia was delighted at the offer, she was convinced that this was a prank call. She was laden with responsibilities at work, and she didn't need to waste her time on false hope. Besides, why would anyone ask her to fly on a mission as dangerous and groundbreaking as this one?

Once Amelia learned that the caller had excellent references, she knew he was telling the truth. It was the greatest opportunity she had ever received. She immediately said yes to the invitation.

She was brought to New York for an interview. In New York, she was told who her copilot would be. His name was Wilmer "Bill" Stultz, and he was a well-known and respected pilot. There would also be another man onboard named Louis E. "Slim" Gordon who was a famous mechanic and Stultz's copilot. If anything went wrong, it would be his responsibility to fix the plane.

On June 17, 1928, the three of them set off on their journey from Trepassey Harbor, Newfoundland, in Canada. They flew in a small plane nicknamed "Friendship." Even though the plane was considered fast at that time, it took them almost twenty-one hours to reach their destination in Great Britain! It was a long, grueling journey, but when they finally arrived in Burry Port, Wales, they were famous. The story of their journey was told all over the world, and Amelia instantly became a celebrity. She could have become haughty or satisfied with her accomplishments. Instead, she wanted to achieve more.

From then on, the sky was the limit for Amelia. She decided to invest all of her time in flying and attempting to set new world records. In 1928, she published a book that was titled *20 Hrs., Forty Min.* It was a perfect title because that was the exact amount of time it took her to complete the journey across the Atlantic Ocean.

In 1929, she was elected as an official for the National Aeronautic Association, and she encouraged the members to create separate flying records for women. She set and broke many of those records herself, including the record for fastest speed in an airplane.

Amelia knew that she had been given a terrific opportunity when she had been asked to fly across the Atlantic Ocean. However, she still desired more. In the original mission, she had flown with two men. This time, she wanted to make the journey on her own. On May 20, 1932, she began her second journey across the Atlantic Ocean. This time she traveled alone, and the trip only took her 14 hours and 56 minutes! It meant that she had become the first woman to ever fly solo across the Atlantic Ocean.

In August of that same year, Amelia isolated herself as the greatest female pilot of her generation. She set a record for speed when she flew all the way across the United States in 19 hours and 5 minutes. In 1933, she made the same flight in 17 hours and 7 minutes, breaking her own record. Two years later, she flew from Oakland, California, to Honolulu, Hawaii, which was a distance of over 2,400 miles (3,862 km).

People of her time period, particularly men, may have been appalled at the idea of a woman as brave as Amelia Earhart accomplishing all these feats. She encouraged people to doubt her. It inspired her to make new and exciting journeys that shocked the world.

When she was nearly forty years old, Amelia wanted to make one last mark on the world of flight. Her goal was to fly a plane around the world. It would be a long journey that would take days, not hours. It was also her most dangerous mission yet.

The trip started well with a successful first leg from California to Hawaii. When she began the second leg, a tire blew, causing severe damage to the plane. The flight was called off. A few months later, Amelia tried again. This time she headed east beginning in Miami, Florida.

For a month, Amelia flew east, making stops in Africa, India, and southeast Asia. When she arrived in New Guinea, she had only one more leg to go, but it was over the vast expanse of the Pacific Ocean. During this leg, she lost communication with the U.S. Coast Guard, and her plane disappeared. A rescue mission was sent to find her. Day after day, rescuers looked for her and her plane, but they found nothing. Sadly, Amelia was never heard from again.

To this day, no one is sure what happened to Amelia or her plane. It was a very sad time for many people who had been inspired by her and all of the challenges she met. Amelia Earhart will always be remembered as someone who changed the world in many ways and never floundered in the face of difficulty. She loved to fly and was a pioneer for women in flight.

Think Critically

1. What characteristics did Amelia possess as a child that may have contributed to her attitude as an adult?

2. How was Amelia a good role model for others?

3. What word from the story indicates that Amelia's first journey across the Atlantic Ocean was a difficult one?

4. Summarize the story of Amelia's life in a few sentences.

5. What do you think was Amelia's greatest accomplishment? Why?

 **Social Studies**

Learn About Aviation Find out more about the history of flight. Who were some other important female pilots? Make a list of them and their accomplishments.

School-Home Connection Share this book with a family member. Then discuss why Amelia was an inspiration to so many.

Word Count: 1,412